Costumes
from the Forbidden City

By ALAN PRIEST
Curator of Far Eastern Art

The Metropolitan Museum of Art

New York, 1945

ARNO PRESS

1974

AUTHOR'S NOTE

For a brief period, from early March to early May, 1945, the Metropolitan Museum is presenting a special exhibition of costumes from the Forbidden City, the walled area in Peking that enclosed the imperial palaces and their appurtenances. The court robes and other Chinese textiles now assembled in the Museum form the largest group ever to be shown together. The scheme of dating by which they are arranged, covering the entire Ch'ing dynasty, is set forth in the following pages. Besides the series of robes of the Manchu court, the exhibition includes Buddhist robes, Taoist robes, and theatrical robes; these are reviewed on pages 14-16. There are also a few important hangings and some insignia ("mandarin squares").   A. P.

CHRONOLOGY

Ming Dynasty	1368-1644
Ch'ing Dynasty	1644-1912
The Emperors	
Shun Chih	1644-1661
K'ang Hsi	1662-1722
Yung Chêng	1723-1735
Ch'ien Lung	1736-1795
Chia Ch'ing	1796-1820
Tao Kuang	1821-1850
Hsien Fêng	1851-1861
T'ung Chih	1862-1874
Kuang Hsü	1875-1908
Hsüan T'ung	1909-1911
The Republic	1912-

(Hsüan T'ung continued his court in the northern part of the Forbidden City until late in 1924.)

Reprinted by permission of the Metropolitan Museum of Art

LC #74-168427
ISBN 0-405-02265-4

Manufactured in the United States of America

An Analysis of the Ch'ing Dynasty Style
Based on Twelve-Symbol Robes

The changes of style in the robes of the imperial court of the Ch'ing dynasty can be understood far better by studying the series of details shown in the accompanying illustrations—the wave borders (figs. 8-11)—the central mountains in the wave borders (figs. 12-15)—the clouds, and particularly the clouds (figs. 4-7)—than they can by verbal description, but it is perhaps worth while to sketch in words the outstanding points for consideration, to offer suggestions, and to open the way for constructive comment and study. This analysis of the Ch'ing dynasty style is based on the scheme of dating derived from a comparison of the robes of Kuo Ch'in Wang, which may be dated 1738 (when he was buried) or earlier, first, with a long series of twelve-symbol imperial robes and, second, with a large number of robes that are obviously associated with them. The scheme, since it was first set forward in 1943, has been in general most favorably received, and no sensible objection has been raised against it. Furthermore, whereas at that time we felt that we could account for the period from late K'ang Hsi (the end of the seventeenth century) through the reign of Tao Kuang, we now feel that we can tentatively extend the period covered right back to Shun Chih (1644-1661), at the beginning of the dynasty, and go a long way towards disentangling the last part of the dynasty, tracing the scheme right down through twenty-odd years of the twentieth century.

The basis of the present study is the huge mass of material in the four most important public collections of Chinese textiles in the country, the Minneapolis Institute of Arts, the William Rockhill Nelson Gallery of Art, Kansas City, the Art Institute of Chicago, and the Metropolitan Museum. Also included are a number of robes from other collections, notably those of Mr. and Mrs. Walter Beck, Mrs. D. Clifford Martin, and the Honorable James W. Gerard.

The robes, some insignia ("mandarin squares"), and a great number of fragments which we all call Ming present the testimony for the dating. There was a time when some of the so-called Lama robes (see page 15) were generally thought to be Ming, and it is possible that some of them are, but at present few would date them earlier than the seventeenth century. So far we have found no secular or court robes that anybody calls Ming. It is therefore probable that the robes dealt with here are almost entirely of the Ch'ing dynasty, and we can try to solve the puzzle of their dating.

SHUN CHIH (1644-1661)

This was the period in which the Manchus, after conquering China, set to work to create a new culture, which was to be a blend of old China and Manchu tradition. In this process, however, as far as the court robes went, they remodeled old China in a manner which must have seemed at the time to conservatives perfectly shocking.

Though we have no actual Ming robes, we can see the voluminous but simple red robes of official dress with their huge and graciously delineated insignia squares in the portraits (a style which the true Chinese families continued often to employ in their private funerary portraits right down to the end of the Ch'ing dynasty), and we can get at least a hint of imperial dress from the portraits in the Forbidden City and from book illustrations. The cut of the imperial robes, like that of the robes of Ming officials, is commodious. In one series of imperial portraits in the Forbidden City the emperors were portrayed in plain yellow, except, possibly, for the dragon insignia on the chest. In the books the imperial robes are shown with huge sleeves and with the lower part of the robe belted in at the waist to give somewhat the appearance of a separate skirt; some separate skirts, also, are illustrated. When the twelve imperial symbols (see pages 7, 8; figs. 2, 3) are shown, they appear to be duplicated at right and left.

The Manchus, on the other hand (and here we have, as well as the portraits, the actual robes), appear in various but quite different attire. The robes are cut close round the neck and quite close under the arms. In the books, the court robes for both sexes are shown with the "horseshoe" cuff, but a number of the actual robes of the less formal type have the wide sleeves of informal Manchu feminine dress. The most common type of imperial robe, called in the sumptuary laws *chi fu* ("auspicious robe"), falls in one straight sweep from neck to hem and is covered with an all-over pattern that was set by law in the main points of its design but varied from emperor to emperor in details, as we shall see. The second type, which we see mostly in formal series of portraits of the emperors, is described in the laws as *ch'ao fu* (literally, "court robe") and was prescribed for formal court functions and special ceremonies at the Altars of Heaven, Earth, Sun, and Moon. I suggest that we call this type robes of state, not only because the "auspicious robes" are what we are used to calling court robes, but to distinguish them from the really informal everyday dress. The emperors' robes of state, instead of falling straight from neck to hem, have an inset waistband to which the skirt is joined, and the fullness of the lower part of the robe falls from darts or pleats. (The empresses's robes of state vary. Some have pleats, like the emperors' robes, and some fall in a straight line from the neck to the hem.) Like the auspicious robes, most of them have a prodigious amount of decoration, but it is quite different in character.

Perhaps it will be helpful to give examples of the sumptuary laws (Kuang Hsü edition) for one of the emperor's auspicious robes and for one of his robes of state. An emperor's *chi fu*, or auspicious robe, is also called a *lung p'ao* ("dragon robe") and under that name is described as follows:

Emperor's Dragon Robe

Color: bright yellow. Collar and cuffs stone black with striped gold edge.

Embroidered design:
   nine gold dragons,
   arranged twelve symbols,
   at intervals five-colored clouds,
   on front and back below collar a front-facing
      dragon (*chêng lung*),
   (on folds) left and right of seam, walking
      dragons,
   on the inner flap a walking dragon,
   on each shoulder a front-facing dragon,
   in the lower border, Eight Precious Things
      set in waves (*li shui*, literally "upright
      water").
Four slits.
(Material): padded — lined — gauze — fur — according to the season.

One of the emperor's *ch'ao fu*, or robes of state, is described as follows:

Emperor's Winter Court Dress, No. 1

Color: bright yellow, except at the sacrifices at the Altar of Heaven and the Temple of Agriculture, when the color is blue.
Spreading collar and lower part of robe surfaced with undyed sable.
Embroidered design:
   on each shoulder, in front (on the chest), and
      on the upper back a five-clawed, front-
      facing dragon;
   in the pleats (on the lower part of the robe),
      six walking dragons (three in front, three
      in the back);
   on the front and back of the upper part of the
      robe, twelve symbols.

In the auspicious robes the design as a whole is usually interpreted as representing the universe. The five-colored clouds in the main field of the robe symbolize heaven; below the clouds is the sea, a pattern of waves and spray mingled with clouds, and amid these waves, at the center front and back and at each side of the robe, are mountains symbolizing earth. The nine imperial dragons may be considered symbols of the emperor in his role as the Son of Heaven, the intermediary between Heaven and Earth, and it is relevant to remember that the dragon is also a symbol of spiritual power and intelligence. A great deal has been written about the flaming jewel or pearl which appears with the dragon, sometimes before him, sometimes in his very clutches, but its exact meaning is still elusive. Perhaps it is a symbol of the very essence of the mind and spirit—the ultimate understanding the dragon's intelligence strives for. Its origins? I don't know: it might go back to the *yin-yang* symbol or the *ch'i* ("vital essence"), or it might be the precious pearl of the Buddhist Eight Precious Things, transposed and transformed by the Chinese. It has also been discussed both as a possible sun symbol and as a moon symbol. (The symbolism of the robes of state is similar to that of the auspicious robes, but the symbols are differently arranged.)

In addition to the decorative elements set down in the sumptuary laws, various Taoist symbols are freely used, together with the Buddhist symbols and flowers with symbolic meanings. Sometimes, too, there are longevity (*shou*) characters, the Buddhist swastika (*wan tzŭ*), double happiness (*shuang hsi*) characters, which are generally associated with marriage, bats, which by a play on words stand for happiness, and cranes, which usually stand for longevity. Still other symbols occasionally appear.

In Western collections the auspicious robes are very many, and the robes of state so far are very, very few. Until recently there were just three emperors' robes of state in well-known public collections, one in the Minneapolis Institute (fig. 54), another in the Metropolitan Museum, and the third in the Honolulu Academy of Arts, all of them dark blue-black and of the type described in the laws as "Emperor's Summer Robe." Lately the Metropolitan has acquired another robe of state, a yellow one with all twelve symbols on it—the first of the kind that has come to light. It is attributed to T'ung Chih (fig. 39). Two other emperors' robes of state belong to Mr. and Mrs. Walter Beck.

The first Ch'ing sumptuary laws of any consequence after the Manchus took Peking were not published until May 14, 1652, and were very incomplete. They were republished with minor

changes from time to time throughout the dynasty. We need somebody to settle down and translate them all. It will be very valuable to have them translated, but it won't decide everything; for at the very best they leave out countless things which may have seemed too obvious and simple to the boards that wrote them down to mention, but which give any hapless curator who attempts to classify the robes on the basis of their stipulations many a headache. For instance, just one of many troubles, and seemingly one that ought to be most easy to solve, is the question of what the sumptuary laws mean when they prescribe "bright" yellow and "golden" yellow. This should be easy. We have a long series of imperial robes that are yellow, and they vary from a kind of greenish yellow to an almost orange yellow. We also have a number which are candidly orange. We can guess that the greenish yellow which we have long associated with imperial China is the "bright" yellow, and we can guess that the pale, clear lining of many of the robes is the "golden" yellow; but there is nowhere in the laws any mention of orange, nor is there any possible way of translating the Chinese words for orange or vermilion into English as either bright or golden yellow. Vice versa, the English word orange can't be translated into Chinese as any manner or degree of yellow. That is the kind of trouble you get into, if you take the sumptuary laws too seriously. The writers of the laws and the weavers of the coats had a certain amount of agreement on general principles, but in practical detail they were about as consistent as a peace conference. The laws are very good as far as they go, but they don't go far enough. Why expect them to? Likewise the portraits, which are often a help. A properly documented series of portraits might well let us follow the main changes of fashion; but to attempt to catalogue Chinese court robes by means of the portraits alone is almost as deliciously silly an idea as it would be to write a history of European lace on the basis of the dabs of white paint with which Rubens and Van Dyck and Watteau presented the illusion of ruffs and cuffs.

The young who venture into the brambles and thickets of Chinese art cannot be too often re-

5

minded to approach it modestly and gently and to keep in mind Mr. Francis Taylor's well-placed warning: ". . . the German passion for classification and spinning a priori theories from artificially established premises . . . set a standard for unintelligibility which has remained in vogue until the present day." Particularly should the young be most wary of laying down the law for the business of disentangling the unsolved mysteries of Chinese textiles, mysteries which are still many. In this field the sumptuary laws are of use and help, but the ultimate proof and secret is inherent in the textiles themselves; and when we get to know them well enough, they will arrange and order themselves in indisputable proof and array. They are well on the way to it already.

Knowing that the period of Shun Chih was a formative period and working back from our clearest landmark, the robes of Kuo Ch'in Wang, buried in 1738, we come to vestiges of Shun Chih and early Ch'ing. By tracing back the sequence of wave and cloud forms we come to one robe (fig. 16) and a considerable number of insignia squares which seem to show quite clearly the beginning of the Ch'ing style. The robe is definitely of Manchu cut and the squares are consistent with it.

The robe which we propose as a Shun Chih robe is unique in our entire series. It is of an extremely heavy tapestry weave, closer to the fragments of tapestry which we believe to be Ming than to the delicate technical perfection of the later tapestry robes and insignia. The proper number of dragons, the wave border, and the five-colored clouds prescribed in the sumptuary laws are there, but the design hasn't even begun to adjust and balance itself into the measured formal pattern which we are accustomed to in the general run of court robes. In this early robe the central dragons on the chest and upper back are huge—much larger than the four on the lower part of the robe. The spaces which in the later robes are filled with clouds and bats and various symbols are in this instance largely filled with a plethora of small dragons and variegated forms of the longevity character, *shou,* giving an effect very reminiscent of the repetitions on Ming robes as seen in book illustra-

tions. The wave border at the hem is very narrow, with simple undulations of waves in which there are no whorls; the clouds in this border wander about, splendid but undisciplined; the central mountains rise in simple spires, very tall and straight, with rather over-size splashes of spray. And, above all, the clouds that appear on the body of the ground are energetic but small—seemingly experiments and closely akin to the fat little knots that appear on the insignia squares of early Ch'ing.

This is a robe which is certainly seductive as illustrating the beginnings of the Ch'ing style. We place it as Shun Chih rather than K'ang Hsi, because it is a full-size man's robe and K'ang Hsi came to the throne as a child of seven, and if we date it as late as the period of K'ang Hsi's maturity, then the formative era of the new dynasty would seem to be extended longer than is likely. This appears on every score to be an experimental robe; let us tentatively ascribe it to Shun Chih, as an early attempt to work out a court robe on the principles set down by the sumptuary laws.

K'ANG HSI (1662-1722)

The next robe to be considered as an early one is certainly considerably later than the robe described above. This later robe (fig. 18), which belongs to the Minneapolis Institute of Art, is of a peculiar shade of yellowish green, almost a chartreuse. Here the balance between dragon and wave border, which was to become the formula for Ch'ing dynasty robes, is already in evidence, but where the spaces in the first robe are filled mostly with dragons, the spaces in this one are filled with clouds—clouds which are exaggerated in size— and, strangely enough, the inner flap, which usually has as its main feature a dragon, has instead a single, enormous cumulous cloud. The wave border at the hem is deeper than that of the first robe; the waves are really beginning to surge, and the horizontal waves are topped by huge whorls. The central mountains and the spray are more complicated than those in the blue robe of Shun Chih, but they have not yet reached the soaring pinnacles of the developed K'ang Hsi robes. This robe might be listed just as a variant of the full K'ang Hsi

6

style but for one arresting feature; on the upper front, on the upper back, and on each shoulder it carries a large, round symbol of the sun. While there may well be a sumptuary law covering such a garment, we have not as yet found it, and the repetition of a single symbol reminds us again of the illustrations of Ming robes and inclines us to pose it as an early robe—early to middle K'ang Hsi at least.

The sun symbol which occurs here is one of the twelve (figs. 2, 3) that hark straight back to the Book of Rites, where they are first mentioned.

I (Yü) wish to see the emblematic figures of the ancients—the sun, the moon, the stars, the mountains, the dragon and the flaming fowl which are depicted on the upper garment; the temple cups, the aquatic grass, the flames, the grains of rice, the hatchet and the symbol of distinction which are embroidered on the lower garment. I wish to see all these displayed with the five colors, so as to form the official robe. (Legge, *Chinese Classics*, vol. III: *Shu Ching*, part 1, p. 80.)

These twelve symbols, described in a memorial on regulations for official costumes by Yang Ch'iung and quoted in the *T'u Shu Chi Ch'êng* ("Encyclopaedia of K'ang Hsi"), have been summarized by Wang Chi-chen as follows:

1, 2, and 3. The Sun, the Moon, and the Constellation, which symbolize the light of the good and wise king shining upon the world.

4. The Mountain, which distributes cloud and rain and thus symbolizes the beneficence of the good and wise king to his people.

5. The Dragon, ever infinite in its changes, which symbolizes the adaptability of the good and wise king, who publishes his laws and instructions according to the needs of the time.

6. The Flowery Bird, with the five colors on its body, which symbolizes the cultured accomplishments of the good and wise king.

7. The Cups, with the representation of the tiger and the long-tailed monkey, which symbolize the fact that the good and wise king pacifies rebellions with supernatural force as the tiger overpowers things with courage and forcefulness. (The original was vague—the writer grouped the tiger and the monkey together as if they signified the same quality, but according to other writers the monkey symbolizes cleverness or cunning, because, having its nose tilted skyward, it has sense enough to stop it up with its long tail, so as to prevent the rain from running into its windpipe.)

8. The Water Weed, which rises and falls with the water, symbolizing the good and wise king responding to the needs of the time.

9. The Millet, upon which the life of human beings depends, symbolizing the good and wise king as the mainstay of all things.

10. The Fire, which fires pottery, melts metals, and cooks, symbolizing the good and wise king's supreme virtue as daily renewed.

11. The Ax, which can cut and sever, symbolizing the decisiveness of the good and wise king when facing situations.

12. The Symbol of Distinction (*fu*), consisting of two *chi* characters back to back, which symbolizes the working together of the prince and his ministers.

In auspicious robes these symbols are usually arranged as follows: in front, the Sun on the wearer's left shoulder, the Moon on the right, the Constellation on the chest, the Ax and the Symbol of Distinction left and right at the height of the lower ribs, the libation Cups and the Water Weed left and right at about the height of the knees; on the back, the Mountain in the center of the shoulder blades, the small paired dragons and the Flowery Bird left and right at the lower angle of the shoulder blades, the Fire and the Millet left and right below the knees. The twelve symbols are used on only one of the Metropolitan's robes of state—the yellow one attributed to T'ung Chih (fig. 39). Here eight of the symbols appear in the same places as on the auspicious robes, and four are dropped to the lower band.

These twelve symbols are not mentioned in the early Ch'ing sumptuary laws, which are very sketchy indeed. They are not mentioned, as far as we can find, until the set of Ch'ing laws published as late as 1759, but as Ch'ien Lung remarked in the preface to his laws that he wished to maintain strictly the precedents of his ancestors ("I follow the past regulations of my dynasty. I dare not change them for fear later generations would hold such an action of mine [as a precedent] and consider [further changes] of the robes and hats"), it would seem to be just one of those items which were so much taken for granted that nobody bothered to set them down. Certainly in the late robes of K'ang Hsi, the robes ascribed to Yung Chêng, and the earliest robes of Ch'ien Lung all twelve symbols appear again and again.

A considerable number of court robes have long been confidently ascribed to the K'ang Hsi period. They fall into two main groups, one of which is certainly earlier than the other. The earlier group shows the achievement of the design at its most vigorous and powerful best. Of these we have six that presumably belonged to imperial consorts (see fig. 17), one of them answering to the description of a robe of state for an empress or an imperial consort of the first rank. If these robes were made for K'ang Hsi's consorts, we can hardly date them much before 1665, the date of his marriage at the age of eleven. In these robes the central front dragon, like that of the Shun Chih robe, is massive. The wave border has deepened and the top tier of horizontal waves rolls into dynamic whorls, four across the front. The oblique waves at the very bottom are beginning to be emphasized and ripple till they fairly crackle with excitement. The clouds in the border are disciplined and blow up in equidistant puffs, which Miss Lindsay Hughes aptly likens to the head of the ju-i, or lucky scepter. The central mountains tower and airy spray flashes out behind them. The clouds on the field of the robes —and it is always in the clouds on the field of the robes that the sequence may be most easily traced—are no longer the vigorous, dumpy little knots or the tiny medusas and polyps of the earlier style. They have become developed into forms suggestive of lively little dragons, and more often than not they are finished off with a sharp little tail that will be lost by the time they reach the period of Ch'ien Lung. And at this point the

clouds are independent and freely spaced. This is the dynasty's strongest period.

Having achieved the main scheme, the designers of the late K'ang Hsi period were free to vary and embellish the achievement; they were free to perfect wonders of technique and to perform miracles of fantasy and color. The difference between middle and late K'ang Hsi is the difference between the stern, noble sweep of Milton's verse and the almost unbearable shimmer and fire of Shelley's. It is the difference between the golden blare of Wagner and the silvery complications of Debussy. There is no less poetry and music in these Chinese vestments of the period of K'ang Hsi. In design, in color, in texture, in execution and conception they are beyond anything else that human beings have ever devised to clothe themselves in.

For the late K'ang Hsi period we have at least six emperor's robes bearing the twelve imperial symbols and two fragments of emperor's robes— a really glittering array. It would be hard to choose among them; they are all miracles of fancy and invention. One, in the collection of the Minneapolis Institute, is made of tapestry with a quiet blue background and has the charming variant of having eight of the twelve symbols dropped into the wave border, each floating on its own ascension of golden clouds (fig. 22). Another twelve-symbol robe (fig. 23), with brilliant but delicately drawn clouds on a jonquil yellow background, belongs to Kansas City (the Metropolitan, Minneapolis, and Beck collections have fragments of an almost identical robe lacking the twelve symbols). A third, in the collection of Mrs. D. Clifford Martin, is embroidered on satin of a clear, pale yellow in a medley of pale pinks and blues. Three more twelve-symbol robes are in the Metropolitan Museum's collection, and all three are of breath-taking technical brilliance. One (fig. 20) is embroidered in vivid colors on a tiny diamond-diaper background, which is not woven but entirely embroidered in yellow upon red gauze—as a sheer feat of embroidery it has no parallel in robes. The other two are tapestry robes which, of their kind, represent technical perfection. As a tour de force of tapestry weaving the one which has a ground wholly composed of vivid, variegated clouds is unique (fig. 21) and in color is almost insulting to the eye (there is a brocaded fragment similar in design which is a soft sheen of pink and green and gold). The other is the sweetest of all the myriad Chinese robes. The ground is powder blue, and the entire design is keyed to it in tender, dusty shades of blue and yellow, green, and faded rose.

This is the series of robes that are fancy free. The underlying strength and power of the mid-K'ang Hsi robes is still there, but whereas in the earlier robes the central dragon on front and back was a good deal larger than the dragons on the lower part of the robes, in these the dragons have come into balance and are more nearly of the same size. The simple, powerful surge of wave and whorl of the earlier robes has changed—the same brilliance of draughtsmanship, the same underlying theme is there, but it is gentler, and instead of having the stark simplicity of the earlier robes it is adorned and played with according to the poetic fancy of the designer. The mountains on these robes rise into delicate pinnacles laced with spray. And the clouds on the body of the robe—the clouds which are the easiest and most striking clue to follow—you can watch the clouds play and change at the end of K'ang Hsi just as you can watch the cirrus formations of real clouds change and bend and dissolve away.

YUNG CHÊNG (1723-1735)

It is audacious to try to isolate for the twelve-year period of Yung Chêng a special style at all. But I think we can do it. Consider it a transition period between the glorious reign of K'ang Hsi and the comparatively stodgy splendor of Ch'ien Lung. The three twelve-symbol robes here ascribed to Yung Chêng might seem a tenuous and flimsy bridge if they were not supported by a goodly number of obviously related robes that lack only the twelve symbols. It wouldn't matter much if we dropped Yung Chêng out and ascribed his twelve-symbol robes to the youthful Ch'ien Lung, but I don't think we need to do that. I think we have him.

We have three robes (see figs. 24, 25) which stylistically follow upon the late K'ang Hsi robes. If we did not have the K'ang Hsi robes, we should praise these extravagantly; but we have that dazzling array, and when we find even three which fall off so abruptly in style and which tie in so closely with the robes of Yung Chêng's brother Kuo Ch'in Wang (see figs. 26-29), who died in 1738, we shall do well to pause and look them over. These three robes are handsome enough, and they are very well executed, but they lack the dash and brilliance of the preceding series. These are the twelve-symbol robes, mind you, which according to the sumptuary laws are listed only for the emperor (there is at least one portrait of an empress wearing the symbols, but even if this is not a gaffe on the part of the painter, it does not change the stylistic evidence). Here it seems worth while to remark that the feature that attracts most publicity in this scheme of dating—the fact that it appears from the groups of twelve-symbol imperial robes that the wearers differed in stature (and the change in size is a point that seems to hold)—is an easy but very minor clue, tucked in at the end and following the theory of stylistic change.

Here, then, we have three robes with all twelve symbols and a mass of supporting robes. They average, of course, a good two inches shorter than the robes which we call late K'ang Hsi. One (fig. 25) shows a startling variant of the formal pattern in its wave border—it all but omits the oblique stripes at the bottom and churns with horizontal waves. We should not know what to do with it if it were not for the fact that one of the Kuo Ch'in Wang robes (fig. 26), although far superior, has a border which does very much the same thing. And there are half a dozen or more robes without the twelve symbols which are obviously sister robes to this one; they belong to the same group. The other two twelve-symbol robes tie in a conventional, direct sequence with those we call late K'ang Hsi, but they have lost most of the liveness of K'ang Hsi. They are grumpy and unwilling, stingy and parsimonious (comparatively). The wave border in these robes is settling down, and the main field is overcrowded with begrudging attempts to follow the K'ang Hsi clouds. The supporting robes vary a good deal; if we did not have the others, some of them would seem very, very good indeed, but in comparison they are a kind of afterglow of the great period. Perhaps it is wrong to quote again the savage encomium of Bland and Backhouse on Yung Chêng, i.e., "the suspicious, querulous and savagely vindictive individual." Was the emperor's mean nature reflected throughout his governmental bureaus?—one is tempted to play with the idea. At any rate, here are robes close to those of Kuo Ch'in Wang and a certain date—1738; they must be considered as belonging to Yung Chêng and as a bridge between K'ang Hsi and Ch'ien Lung.

CH'IEN LUNG (1736-1795)

There were only twelve years of Yung Chêng and there were a good sixty years of Ch'ien Lung. It is to be expected that the style of the beginning of each reign would follow closely the style of the preceding reign and that if there were changes they would come later, after the new emperor was established. Ch'ien Lung put himself down on record as intending to follow tradition. And with a long reign we should expect a long series of twelve-symbol robes. Which is just what we find. There are some eight or nine at hand (see figs. 30, 32, 33), and we know of many others in public and private collections. We had hoped to be able by now to work out an indisputable sequence of the Ch'ien Lung robes, early, middle, and late. But we cannot yet do that with any security, so we leave the problem open. We can, however, point out the general trend.

There are a number of robes that pivot around the Kuo Ch'in Wang robes of 1738. These might be put either into the end of Yung Chêng or into early Ch'ien Lung. But when we deal with the twelve-symbol robes we find that those in the extensive series belonging to Ch'ien Lung are cut tremendously long and that they have as the most striking difference from earlier groups unusually long oblique wave stripes in the lower border. Now look: nobody knew, until the emperor died, who

was to be the next emperor. His first robes were bound to be like those of his predecessor, and when suddenly we find a whole series of very long robes, whose salient feature is the elongation of the oblique wave stripes of the lower border, it looks very much as if the designers, abruptly faced with a bean-pole emperor, hastily added four or five inches to the hem and let the matter go at that. Once these elongated, oblique stripes at the hem appear, they stay.

It is not only these features, it is the whole pattern and design that change. If the Yung Chêng robes fell off from the grandeur and fantasy of K'ang Hsi, the Ch'ien Lung robes, gorgeous as they are, rapidly settled down to a stereotyped and comparatively very dull formula. The early Ch'ien Lung robes are surely those that come closest to the Yung Chêng and Kuo Ch'in Wang robes. The early robes do, in fact, tie in with Yung Chêng, particularly in the over-all cloud pattern, but whereas the field of the Yung Chêng robes is crowded with clouds, in the Ch'ien Lung robes whole series of clouds are tied together with tiny ribbons—the cloud pattern gets tight and set. In the twelve-symbol robes of Yung Chêng's time the clouds are spindly and tend to weave back and forth from left to right like cowpaths on a steep mountainside. But Kuo Ch'in Wang's Crane and Gate robe, which belongs to the Minneapolis collection, is covered with fat little puffballs of cloud. (The whole Kuo Ch'in Wang series of robes is on a superior level to that of the robes of the Emperor Yung Chêng; the prince's designers were apparently allowed more freedom than were those of the official imperial robes. Miss Hughes gave an excellent description of the prince's robes in the *Gazette des Beaux-Arts* for September, 1943, so we need not diverge here save for particular references.) In almost no time at all the Ch'ien Lung clouds become hybrids of the Yung Chêng horizontal clouds and Kuo Ch'in Wang's puffballs. (Note, however, that the blue and white twelve-symbol robe in the Minneapolis collection has a crowded field, like Yung Chêng's robes, but harks clear back to late K'ang Hsi.) Very, very soon the Ch'ien Lung clouds settle into chains of nice little lumps joined together in series

10

by short-length ribbons. Once set, this type of cloud continues through the dynasty.

At some time during the dynasty background patterns of diapers were introduced, as well as quatrefoils, sometimes with flowers in the center, sometimes with swastikas, and a swastika meander. In one of the K'ang Hsi robes there is a tiny diamond-diaper pattern, Kuo Ch'in Wang had a delicate quatrefoil robe, and in the supporting Yung Chêng robes there are a number with an all-over tendril pattern, so the appearance of these elements in Ch'ien Lung's robes may have been quite early. However, the Ch'ien Lung robes in which the quatrefoil and swastika meander appear, handsome as they are, are comparatively dull and lifeless.

It is apparent, also, that the lower border has been regimented and formalized. When the oblique wave stripes lengthened, the horizontal rolling waves shrunk. The noble surge of the K'ang Hsi waves on Minneapolis's twelve-symbol robe, the fantasy hurricanes on Kuo Ch'in Wang's Hundred Cranes robe in the Kansas City collection, and the waves in the whole enchanting supporting series, which roll and dance clear to the hem over and over again for all the world like Debussy's sea music—these give way to a comparatively narrow band which is as tame as the cascades in Radio City. When it comes to the mountains of the lower border, one finds that the airy spires of late K'ang Hsi have dwindled and become simplified during the transitional period of Yung Chêng. By Ch'ien Lung they have become formal, stalwart blocks and the spray which appears about them has lost the fantastical freedom of the K'ang Hsi robes—and the waves are disciplined almost into the mechanical regularity of the electrically propelled waves in some of our modern swimming pools. The hurricane-wave pattern appears in a number of Ch'ien Lung robes that lack the twelve symbols (see fig. 31). Splendid in itself, the Ch'ien Lung version is nevertheless exaggerated and coarse in comparison with those on robes of the Yung Chêng and Kuo Ch'in Wang series.

Aside from the robes, we have a number of dated Ch'ien Lung textiles. There is no doubt about Ch'ien Lung textiles any longer. Magnificent as they are, they seem dull and set when we compare them with K'ang Hsi textiles (cf. figs. 49, 55, 56). We used to think that textile art came to its peak in Ch'ien Lung and then suddenly fell off in the nineteenth century. It isn't true. The textiles, like the porcelains and like the paintings, were in the Ch'ing dynasty at their best in K'ang Hsi. They did not fall off suddenly in the nineteenth century; they got formal and set in the eighteenth century, and slowly and gently deteriorated. This is the grand scheme. But when we deal with Chinese things, as Mr. Berenson once remarked, even the tenth-rate things are first-rate; it is only when they are put in a series that we see that the late ones are mere ghosts and shadows of a former glory.

CHIA CH'ING (1796-1820)

To this emperor we ascribe a series of robes (see figs. 34, 35) that follow closely upon those of Ch'ien Lung. When these robes are shown in squads, it can be seen at first glance that this series is very much shorter than the Ch'ien Lung robes and, amusingly enough, there are two robes which are identical except for the length of the oblique wave stripes. Of course the shorter robe may have been tampered with; it may be a cut-down Ch'ien Lung robe. Nevertheless, the first Chia Ch'ing robes should logically have been exactly like those of Ch'ien Lung. It takes time for a new period to develop a style, and we have enough of the later robes of Chia Ch'ing to get him down cold. It is clouds again and the oblique wave stripes at the bottom that do it. Once the long oblique wave stripes got into the pattern they stayed, and in this series of shorter robes the proportion of the whole robe changes: the upper part shortens perceptibly and the long wave stripes stay. In the twelve-symbol robes the background becomes much more aggressive. A heavy swastika-meander background is common, and the all-over, crowded Ch'ien Lung clouds have dissolved into floating fragments; after a whole century they are freely spaced again, but not very sensibly spaced, and they are far more suggestive of polliwogs and newts than their dragon-cloud ancestors of K'ang Hsi and Yung Chêng. The mountains, also, are becoming shorter and even more blocky than those of Ch'ien Lung.

And in these robes there begin to appear dabs and touches of a particularly vicious violet color which has long been a clue to nineteenth-century textiles. This appears first in Chia Ch'ing. It is not like the earlier violets and purples; unlike most purple, it fades reluctantly. We do not know what this dye is. We are to date pitifully ignorant of dyes. This is not the time or occasion to diverge into the subject, but it is necessary to make a few succinct observations about aniline dyes. Aniline dyes, invented in the fifties, never reached China at all until after 1875; they could not be bought in Peking or Tientsin as late as the early 1920's. It is very doubtful that they were ever used by the notably conservative imperial factories. When you deal with court robes, don't worry at all about aniline until after 1875, and you probably needn't worry much then. What is certain is that in the first quarter of the nineteenth century the Chinese somewhere invented or imported a bright purple dye which fades slowly. It is not an aniline dye; an aniline purple, exposed, will vanish in a scant three years. We don't know what the Chinese dye is, but it appears suddenly and thereafter is a positive clue to nineteenth-century Chinese textiles when it is used in them.

TAO KUANG (1821-1850)

Whereas in the Chia Ch'ing robes we find experimental dabs of this bright purple, in the Tao Kuang robes it begins to run riot.

The Tao Kuang robes, which closely follow the Chia Ch'ing robes in style, are much bigger and longer (see figs. 36, 37). The oblique wave pattern, which first became extended in Ch'ien Lung and which persisted in Chia Ch'ing and caused the upper part of the robe to shrink a little, is continued in Tao Kuang as part of the inherent design. And the stripes become still longer and straighter. The upper part of the robe shrinks still more. In mid-K'ang Hsi these oblique waves scarcely reached the ankle of the wearer, in Yung Chêng they began to be emphasized a little, in Ch'ien Lung they took a startling leap in length which continued through Chia Ch'ing, and in Tao Kuang they shot up all the way to the knee. The Tao Kuang clouds follow closely those of Chia Ch'ing; they vary and lengthen a little bit, but it would be difficult to make clear the difference.

Luckily, among the Tao Kuang robes there are two which have a startling variant of the wild-wave border (see fig. 37)—a turmoil of waves intershot with patches of oblique waves. Just as we could liken the hurricane-wave robe of Yung Chêng to the dated Hundred Cranes robe of Kuo Ch'in Wang, we find that we can match the border of the Tao Kuang robe to the wave border of a hanging in the Minneapolis collection (fig. 38), which is dated the fifteenth year of Tao Kuang—1835. This is heaven-sent. It gives us the second landmark— first there is Kuo Ch'in Wang and 1738, and then Tao Kuang and 1835. It ties the whole central sequence together incontrovertibly.

The Tao Kuang robes feature the swastika-meander backgrounds with an emphasis on longevity characters interspersed. The color combinations are gaudy and often exciting. There are two with a deep shell-pink background, and one or two confined to a combination of green and yellow that are as lovely as a late August afternoon. Don't sneer at the nineteenth century.

HSIEN FÊNG (1851-1861)

For the brief twelve years of Hsien Feng's reign we have not a thing in the imperial robes that we can put a finger on. We think, and it is pure guess, that there was very little change in style. There are quite a lot of robes of the Tao Kuang style at hand; it is possible that some of them are actually Hsien Fêng, but we are not yet prepared to say so. We do, however, group a series of robes which go dizzy with color and vary slightly in height as possibly of the period of Hsien Fêng.

T'UNG CHIH, KUANG HSÜ, HSÜAN T'UNG

With T'ung Chih (1862-1874) we know that, for the first time since K'ang Hsi, there was a child emperor. And for him we have a robe of state that dovetails with the Tao Kuang series. This robe (fig. 39) is so close in style to its predecessors that, in spite of the fact that Hsien Fêng was followed by three child emperors, there is a very good chance that it is indeed T'ung Chih's. Better yet, we have a small jacket with the same cloud pattern, which was made as a temple offering and dated the ninth year of T'ung Chih. So we can present our series with some assurance right down to about 1870.

From 1875 on we cannot yet offer a clear sequence, but only suggestions to be considered. We have, for instance, a robe with a blue ground and dragons embroidered in seed pearls and coral which fits the description offered by the sumptuary laws for a robe for an empress dowager or an empress (fig. 40). We have no right to say that this belonged to Tz'ŭ Hsi, but there is a possibility that it was hers—she did not attain the title of empress dowager until 1861. The wave border of this robe is worked in very finely wrapped gold and silver thread (it breaks and cracks easily). This type of gold and silver appears in quite a lot of robes. May we not try it out for T'ung Chih or even Kuang Hsü?

A dated Kuang Hsü hanging in Minneapolis has an inscription that reads: "On a lucky day of the eleventh month of the thirteenth year of Kuang Hsü," and so forth (the thirteenth month is in concordance with December 15, 1887, to January 12, 1888). An interesting feature of this hanging is that the gold and silver threads are couched with threads of different colors. We have robes and squares that are worked in the same technique. So may we not suggest that first we get plain gold and silver and then get gold and silver touched up with colored thread?

There is another clue which comes up at the end of the century. This is in a robe which the late Miss Carl, who painted the famous portrait of the Empress Dowager Tz'ŭ Hsi, told us certainly belonged to her (fig. 41), and it is very, very like the robes Tz'ŭ Hsi is shown wearing in her photographs. The best clue comes in the use of patches of narrow and rather shadowy gold and grayish silver oblique wave stripes. This lets us put close to 1900 a number of court robes (see fig. 42) and insignia squares which have the same decoration. How much earlier than 1900 we cannot yet say.

Hsüan T'ung (1909-1911), of course, reigned only three years before the revolution, but he continued his court in Peking until 1924. We can't see enough in the photographs to be dogmatic about a style for him, but there are enough people who knew him and a number who must actually have documented robes from him to clear up that question when we can coax them to come forward and tell us. From the photographs it looks as if the style cheapened and coarsened. We have two robes with five-clawed dragons—one red, one mulberry in ground—that must have belonged to the court of the latter part of Kuang Hsü's reign (1875-1908) or to the court of Hsüan T'ung. Another of this type, in blue brocade, is in the Minneapolis collection (fig. 44). In these robes we find the final decay of the whole grand scheme of design set up at the time of K'ang Hsi. The polliwog clouds, that first appear in Chia Ch'ing and are still used as late as T'ung Chih, have become coarse, careless splotches, scalloped and knicked. The wave border at the hem is a mere sketch of its former brilliance. The central mountains have dwindled to blocks and the symbols, which were once the Eight Precious Things, have become a smattering of cranes, vases, gates, and military implements for which as yet no sumptuary law has been found nor a sensible explanation offered.

And in the midst of these scattered items there is a painted sketch for an emperor's twelve-symbol robe (fig. 43)—a small one, employing a great deal of pale purple. This must be a cartoon for a boy's robe—for either the boy Kuang Hsü or the boy Hsüan T'ung; which one we hope eventually to find out.

13

Priest Robes and Theatrical Robes

BUDDHIST ROBES

The Buddhist priest robes are of several types, but all are cut either in an elongated rectangle or in a variant of this rectangle which is shaped to fit under the right arm (see fig. 45). These robes are worn in a manner somewhat suggestive of the Roman toga. They are draped over the left shoulder and under the right arm, where they fall in a vertical line; to hold them in place, they are fastened in front below the left shoulder by a cord, a ring, and a buckle in the shape of a *ju-i* ("lucky scepter"). However rich and gorgeous the material employed, the robes are either actually composed of small squares sewed together, or woven to represent squares, or divided by superimposed bands to represent squares—a symbolic representation of the rags which Buddha wore. We have a fairly recent clear red robe that originally belonged to the Abbot Li Hai of the monastery of Chieh T'ai Ssŭ and that since 1934 has been the property of Li Lung. It was worn over a flame-colored underrobe with huge sleeves tailored so that the points just reached the hem of the robe. The abbot wore these vestments at most Buddhist ceremonies in the decade between 1925 and 1935, presumably just as his predecessors had done for centuries before. The attendant monks usually wore gray coats and toga-like robes of a faded rose color.

Besides the comparatively plain robes, there are a number of incredibly gorgeous tapestry robes. In these the small squares are not only decorated with flowers (the *pao hsiang hua*, "precious image flower") but have as their main feature a large central panel bearing the imperial five-clawed dragon. Were these reserved for the actual use of the emperor when he chose to take part in a Buddhist service, or could they be used by the abbots of monasteries under imperial patronage?

One particularly interesting series of Buddhist robes was made for the theater. These robes, shaped to fit under the arm, are composed of squares of brocade of myriad patterns, but one brocade with a tendril pattern in gold runs through all of them. These robes will be referred to again when we speak of theatrical robes, because luckily the same bolts of brocade which appear here in large and handsome squares appear again and again in another extensive series of theatrical robes and tie both lots together.

There were at least eight and perhaps more Buddhist robes of this type on the Peking market in 1929. Two are now in the Metropolitan collection, a third in the Minneapolis collection, a fourth in private hands. The others may eventually turn up. When they first appeared, the Chinese authority on the Chinese theater, Professor Ch'i Ju-shan, dated them as at least Ch'ien Lung, and I now think that we can date them late K'ang Hsi. After all, the twelve-year bridge between late K'ang Hsi and early Ch'ien Lung is nothing to break your heart over, but my thesis is for late K'ang Hsi.

TAOIST ROBES

The Taoist robes are usually almost square, with one side slashed to the middle and there shaped into a collar, so that when the robe is worn the effect is a good deal like that of the old-fashioned army poncho, the kind worn before the war of 1914. Of these robes, one type was commonly seen in and about Peking in the decade of 1925 to 1935. Some are dappled all over with symbols and flowers, mostly rather crude, and are very bright and gay. Others, similar in cut, with a large design composed of the eight diagrams and the *yin-yang* symbol, may or may not be theatrical robes. A magnificent example of this type, dating from the K'ang Hsi period and bearing the imperial dragons, was presented to the Metropolitan Museum by Miss Florance Waterbury (fig. 46). It appears to be an actual ritual robe, not a theatrical robe.

Another type of Taoist robe has wide sleeves and is sometimes divided horizontally by a belt-like band, sometimes not. Such robes are usually ankle length. One which belongs to the Minneapolis collection (fig. 48) has an inscription that reads: "In the eleventh year of the Hsien Fêng period (1861) Chang Yün-lung of the Su Hsing T'ang (hall) ordered and provided [it]." Another, in the Metropolitan collection, is inscribed: "Made by the Ch'êng T'ai Chuang (Success and Prosperity Shop) in the first winter month of the *kuei mao* cyclical year of Kuang Hsü (1903); ordered by Ch'ang Shêng-liu, Ch'ang Shêng-t'an, Ch'ang Shêng-shê of Ch'ien I (district)." This type of robe is described by De Groot as the secondary vestment of a *sai kang* (*shih kung*). It is obviously some kind of secondary Taoist robe.

A third type of priest robe, which at present appears to be Taoist, is cut blanketwise in the usual way and is characterized by a huge square, with other symbols, on the back. On the square is a pagoda surrounded by varying numbers of disks which we believe to have some connection with the stars and planets but for which we have as yet no explanation. Flying cranes and three little gates are often placed at the top of the square, and inside it or on the shoulders there are usually the symbols of the sun and moon. Usually, too, there is a series of four or more cabalistic symbols which we do not as yet understand.

Robes of this type have for the last twenty years and more been called Lama robes. One of the theories advanced by B. Vuilleumier about these robes is that they were worn by the emperor when officiating as the head of the Lama church. There is, however, a portrait of Ch'ien Lung that shows him so officiating, but dressed in orthodox Lama robes. A number of people have seen robes of the type in question stored in what seemed to be strictly a Lama temple. Now we have two such robes with inscriptions. One, on a robe in the Metropolitan collection, reads: "Ordered by Hsü Êrh-kao of the Ming Traveling Palace in the peach (third) month of the fifth year of Chia Ch'ing (April 13-May 11, 1820)." But this does not place the robe in a religion. The second, on a robe in the Minneapolis collection (fig. 47), reads: "Ch'ien Lung, eleventh year, a winter month (1746), Lung Hu Shan (Dragon Tiger Mountain)—Chen Jên Fu, Chang." Now a Chen Jên Fu seems to be the head of a

leading Taoist monastery, if not of the whole Taoist church. Giles translates it as Taoist Pope, but I am not sure that this is not going a little too far. De Groot, describing an inferior example of this type of robe, calls it the "principal vestment of a *sai kang* (*shih kung*)" and would have us believe that such robes were used, not by orthodox priests, but by a cult of Taoist sorcery (*wu*) which dates right straight back to a time before Taoism was so called and had its roots way back in the supernatural origins of the eight diagrams. He would also have us believe that the cult was very secret and, though officially frowned on, was practiced by the best people. It is true that a wonderful lot of astrologers are still practicing in China, but I never saw them turn up in any such robes as these; my stay, however, was under the Republic, and maybe they used them secretly. When we find one of these robes assigned to one of the heads, if not the supreme head, of the Taoist church, it is a good reminder of how ignorant we are of the details of Taoist practice and dress. It would seem that we must give up the idea that they are an imperial form of Lamaism or strictly imperial at all. I had thought that they might be a special form of robe used in the Forbidden City by both religions—one must remember that quantities of them, as was mentioned before, were stored in the Lama temple of the Tzu Ning Kung Hua Yuan ("The Flower Garden of the Palace of Peace and Repose"), which was assigned, like the palace south of it, to retired consorts of the emperor—but at the present writing, with the Minneapolis inscription, we must call them Taoist and leave the question of orthodox or sorcerer Taoist as an open forum.

THEATRICAL ROBES

In a land where the court itself was gorgeous, the theater must needs outdo itself in order to separate itself from the mundane, and by exaggerating the contours of the garments, pitching the color scheme to its fullest violence, and employing large and vivid design, the Chinese theater succeeds admirably and achieves what might be described as architectonic design. In the modern theater—and probably in the ordinary theater of past years—the materials employed are cheap but the result is consistent and, on the stage with its artificial lighting, entirely successful.

Like most of us, the court loved the theater—at some times more than others, apparently. It was common practice to turn over old court robes for use in the Lama-temple devil dances, and it seems evident that the court remade many of its own robes for its own theater. We have the indisputable record of the Empress Dowager Tz'ŭ Hsi—photographs of her appearing as Kuan Yin—and she was probably not the first of the imperial family to play a role on the stage.

If we don't collect recent theatrical robes, soon they are going to become rare. By a miracle one whole theatrical storage appeared on the Peking market as early as 1929, and the Metropolitan Museum was lucky enough to acquire a considerable body of it. More has appeared in the Minneapolis collection, and the rest is scattered far and wide—a considerable amount has already been recognized in European collections. This material now seems to be from the theater of late K'ang Hsi rather than that of early Ch'ien Lung, as was formally supposed. With it we are able for the first time to see what the theater of the imperial court under K'ang Hsi must have been in its full splendor.

Carefully preserved and in their full freshness of color and texture, these robes are extraordinary in workmanship and design, and some of them are stamped with the seal of the imperial theater. The series that we call court ladies runs to at least twelve (the Metropolitan has nine such robes, Minneapolis one coat). These costumes are like nothing else that we have ever seen from China. The skirts are abnormally full, the sleeves sweeping and in great triangles. Broadly and vividly designed—scarlet with a scroll of fêng huangs outlined with gold, green with a pattern of jewels as shining almost as the actual stones, pale gray with a great sweep of fêng huang feathers (fig. 50)—these are the garments by which the ladies of the court are represented. Like the Kuo Ch'in Wang

robes, they are so spectacular that they invite individual names: the Fêng Huang robe, the Red Fêng Huang and Precious Flower robe, the Dragon Grapevine robe (see fig. 51), the Green Jewel robe, the Black Dragon robe (see fig. 51), the Red Dragon robe, the White Dragon robe, the White-Diapered robe, the Yellow and Black Diamond-Checkered robe—a splendid and enchanting array.

A dazzling combination of checks in salmon pink and blue and black, embroidered with clusters of flowers, is used for a costume to represent a Taoist, whose ceremonial robes are gay enough in everyday life and on the stage must be even gaudier. The magnificent needlepoint robe in the collection of Louis V. Ledoux is also, in our opinion, a theatrical robe for a Taoist. It is certainly one of the court theatrical robes, and the large medallions of bats suggest the Taoist symbolism. Neither this robe nor two others of the same type in the Metropolitan collection are representations of ceremonial robes, but rather of the daily costume of Taoist priests, or Followers of the Way. The brocades of various colors which appear in large squares in the stamped theatrical priest robes are also used in details of many of the other theatrical robes.

The representation of court armor in the warrior robes is skillful and effective, with their panels of heavy, looped gold thread or of an interlacing design of embroidery representing chain armor and bits of varicolored brocade for an edging of tigers' claws. In some instances the robes are studded with buttons of eighteenth-century glass. One warrior robe made of imported velvet with panels of imported brocade is embroidered and appliquéd with the usual exaggerated warrior motifs of the Chinese theater, resulting in a magnificent incongruity.

The Metropolitan Museum has six of these warrior robes, four with couched gold thread, one of foreign velvet (the bets are on Russian velvet), and one of black satin (fig. 53). The mate to our red velvet robe is in the Minneapolis collection, a yellow satin robe belongs to Nasli Heeramaneck, and a jacket to Miss Jane Grant. Other similar robes are known here and in Europe.

1. Twelve-symbol emperor's robe, late K'ang Hsi period. Silk tapestry (*k'o ssŭ*). The Metropolitan Museum. Bequest of William Christian Paul, 1930

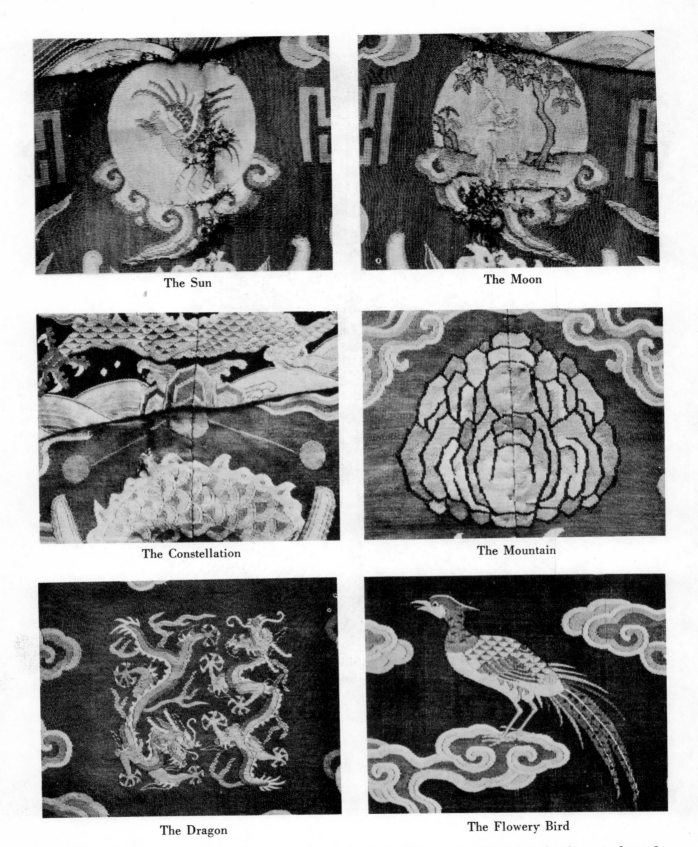

The Sun

The Moon

The Constellation

The Mountain

The Dragon

The Flowery Bird

2. Six of the twelve imperial symbols mentioned in the Book of Rites. Details of the robe shown in figure 1

The Cups

The Water Weed

The Millet

The Fire

The Ax

The Symbol of Distinction

3. Six of the twelve imperial symbols mentioned in the Book of Rites. Details of the robe shown in figure 1

Early Ch'ing (Shun Chih?) insignia square

Shun Chih silk tapestry robe

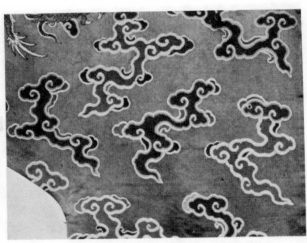

Shun Chih silk tapestry robe

Early to middle K'ang Hsi brocaded satin consort robe

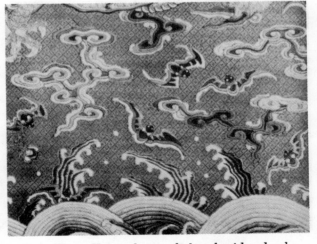

K'ang Hsi brocaded satin consort robe

Late K'ang Hsi twelve-symbol embroidered robe

4. Details showing the development of cloud forms, Shun Chih to K'ang Hsi periods

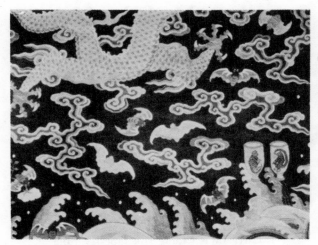

Late K'ang Hsi twelve-symbol silk tapestry robe

Late K'ang Hsi twelve-symbol silk tapestry robe

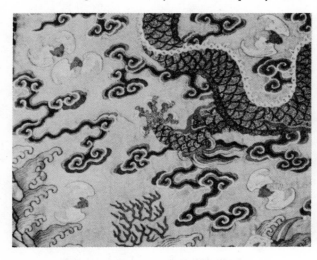

Yung Chêng twelve-symbol silk tapestry robe

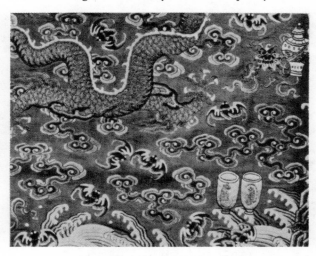

Yung Chêng twelve-symbol embroidered robe

Yung Chêng twelve-symbol silk tapestry robe

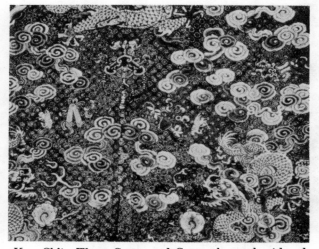

Kuo Ch'in Wang Crane and Gate robe, embroidered

5. Details showing the development of cloud forms, K'ang Hsi to Kuo Ch'in Wang periods

Kuo Ch'in Wang Wave and Pine Tree robe,
embroidered

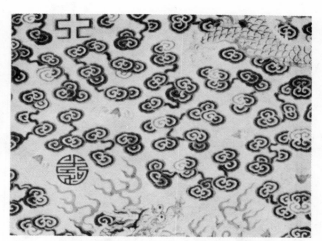

Early Ch'ien Lung silk tapestry robe

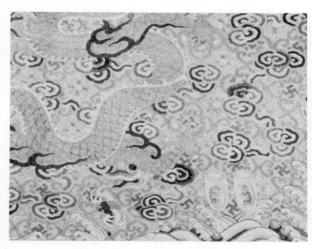

Ch'ien Lung silk tapestry robe

Ch'ien Lung embroidered robe

Chia Ch'ing embroidered robe

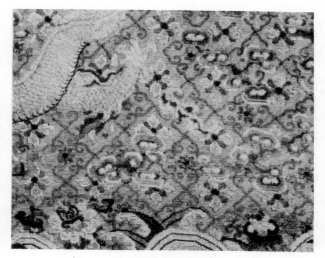

Chia Ch'ing embroidered robe

6. Details showing the development of cloud forms, Kuo Ch'in Wang to Chia Ch'ing periods

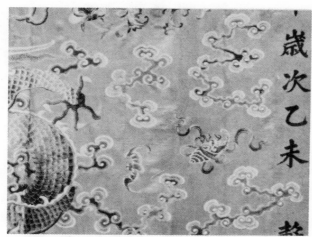 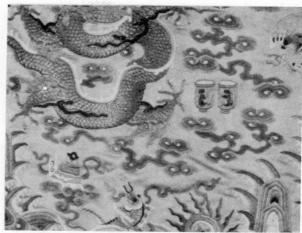

Tao Kuang embroidered hanging, dated 1835   Tao Kuang twelve-symbol embroidered robe

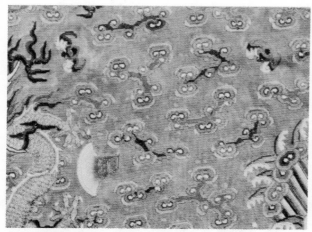 

T'ung Chih twelve-symbol robe of state, embroidered   Pearl and Coral robe, embroidered, T'ung Chih
or Kuang Hsü

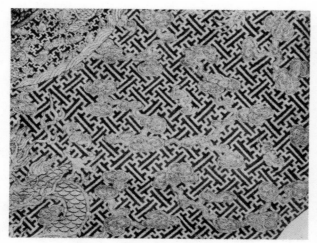 

Kuang Hsü silk tapestry robe   Late Kuang Hsü or Hsüan T'ung brocaded twill robe

7. Details showing the development of cloud forms, Tao Kuang to Hsüan T'ung periods

Early Ch'ing (Shun Chih?) insignia square

Shun Chih silk tapestry robe

Early to middle K'ang Hsi brocaded satin consort robe

Late K'ang Hsi twelve-symbol embroidered robe

Late K'ang Hsi twelve-symbol silk tapestry robe

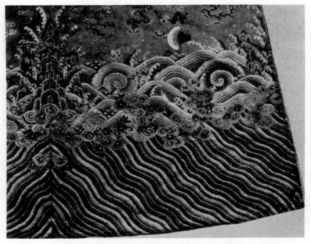

Yung Chêng embroidered robe

8. Details showing the development of wave forms, Shun Chih to Yung Chêng periods

Yung Chêng twelve-symbol tapestry robe

Kuo Ch'in Wang Wave and Pine Tree robe,
embroidered

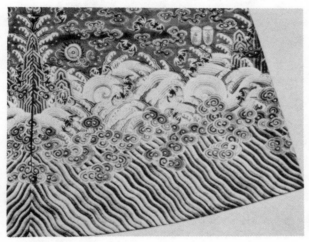

Yung Chêng twelve-symbol embroidered coat

Kuo Ch'in Wang Cloud and Wave robe, embroidered

Yung Chêng twelve-symbol silk tapestry robe

Early Ch'ien Lung twelve-symbol silk tapestry robe

9. Details showing the development of wave forms, Yung Chêng to Ch'ien Lung periods

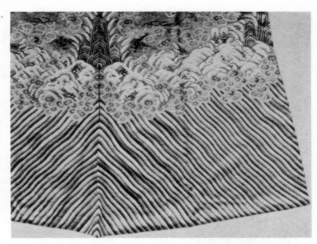

Ch'ien Lung twelve-symbol silk tapestry robe, quatrefoil background

Ch'ien Lung twelve-symbol embroidered robe

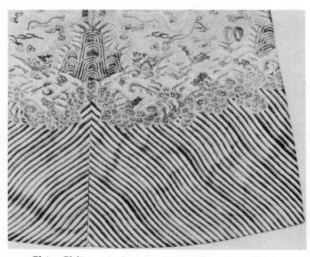

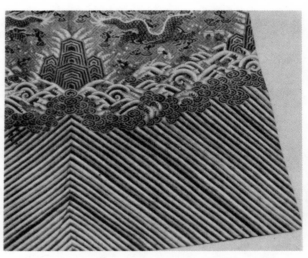

Chia Ch'ing twelve-symbol embroidered robe

Chia Ch'ing twelve-symbol silk tapestry robe

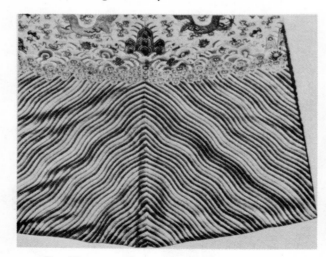

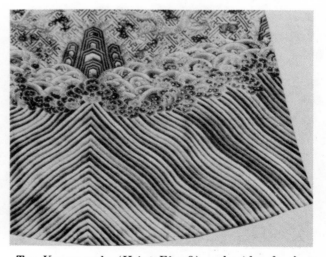

Tao Kuang twelve-symbol embroidered robe

Tao Kuang style (Hsien Fêng?) embroidered robe

10. Details showing the development of wave forms, Ch'ien Lung to Tao Kuang periods

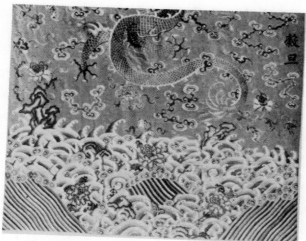

Tao Kuang embroidered hanging, dated 1835

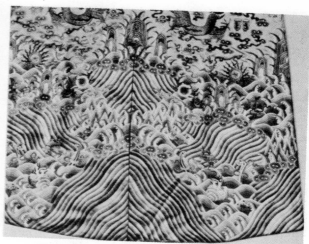

Tao Kuang twelve-symbol embroidered robe

T'ung Chih twelve-symbol robe of state, embroidered

Pearl and Coral robe, embroidered, T'ung Chih or Kuang Hsü

Kuang Hsü silk tapestry robe

Late Kuang Hsü or Hsüan T'ung brocaded twill robe

11. Details showing the development of wave forms, Tao Kuang to Hsüan T'ung periods

Early Ch'ing (Shun Chih?) insignia square

Shun Chih silk tapestry robe

Early to middle K'ang Hsi brocaded satin consort robe

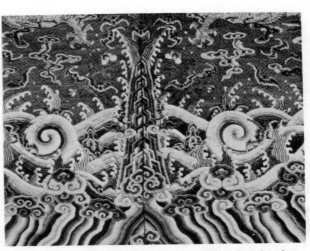

Late K'ang Hsi twelve-symbol embroidered robe

Late K'ang Hsi twelve-symbol silk tapestry robe

Yung Chêng embroidered robe

12. Details showing the development of mountain forms, Shun Chih to Yung Chêng periods

Yung Chêng twelve-symbol silk tapestry robe

Yung Chêng twelve-symbol embroidered coat

Kuo Ch'in Wang Crane and Gate robe, embroidered

Yung Chêng embroidered robe

Kuo Ch'in Wang Cloud and Wave robe, embroidered

Yung Chêng twelve-symbol silk tapestry robe

13. Details showing the development of mountain forms, Yung Chêng to Kuo Ch'in Wang periods

Early Ch'ien Lung twelve-symbol silk tapestry robe

Ch'ien Lung twelve-symbol embroidered robe

Ch'ien Lung twelve-symbol embroidered robe

Chia Ch'ing twelve-symbol silk tapestry robe

Tao Kuang twelve-symbol embroidered robe

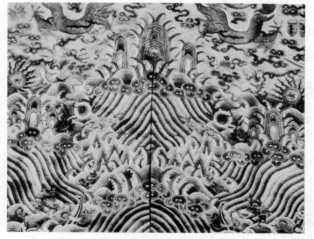

Tao Kuang twelve-symbol embroidered robe

14. Details showing the development of mountain forms, Ch'ien Lung to Tao Kuang periods

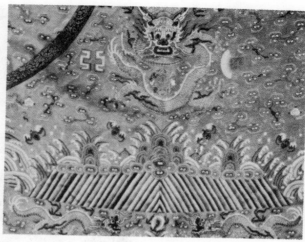

Tao Kuang style (Hsien Fêng?) embroidered robe

T'ung Chih twelve-symbol robe of state, embroidered

Pearl and Coral robe, embroidered, T'ung Chih or
Kuang Hsü

Kuang Hsü silk tapestry robe

Late Kuang Hsü or Hsüan T'ung brocaded twill robe

Hsüan T'ung silk tapestry robe

15. Details showing the development of mountain forms, Hsien Fêng to Hsüan T'ung periods

16. Imperial robe, attributed to Shun Chih period. Silk tapestry (*k'o ssŭ*). The Metropolitan Museum. Bequest of William Christian Paul, 1930

17. Consort robe, early to middle K'ang Hsi period. Brocaded satin. The Minneapolis Institute of Arts

18. Imperial robe with four sun symbols, K'ang Hsi period. Brocaded silk. The Minneapolis Institute of Arts

19. Detail of the inner flap of the sun-symbol robe shown in figure 18

20. Twelve-symbol emperor's robe, late K'ang Hsi period. Embroidered gauze.   The Metropolitan Museum. Purchase, Joseph Pulitzer Fund, 1935

21. Twelve-symbol emperor's robe, late K'ang Hsi period. Silk tapestry (*k'o ssŭ*). The Metropolitan Museum. Purchase, Rogers Fund, 1932

22. Twelve-symbol emperor's robe, late K'ang Hsi period. Silk tapestry (*k'o ssŭ*). The Minneapolis Institute of Arts

23. Twelve-symbol emperor's robe, late K'ang Hsi period. Silk tapestry (*k'o ssŭ*). William Rockhill Nelson Gallery of Art, Kansas City

24. Twelve-symbol emperor's robe, Yung Chêng period. Silk tapestry (*k'o ssŭ*). The Metropolitan Museum. Purchase, Joseph Pulitzer Fund, 1935

25. Twelve-symbol imperial robe, hurricane wave variant, Yung Chêng period. Silk tapestry (*k'o ssŭ*). The Minneapolis Institute of Arts

26. Wave and Pine Tree or Hundred Cranes robe, from the tomb of Kuo Ch'in Wang (d. 1738). Brocaded satin, embroidered. William Rockhill Nelson Gallery of Art, Kansas City

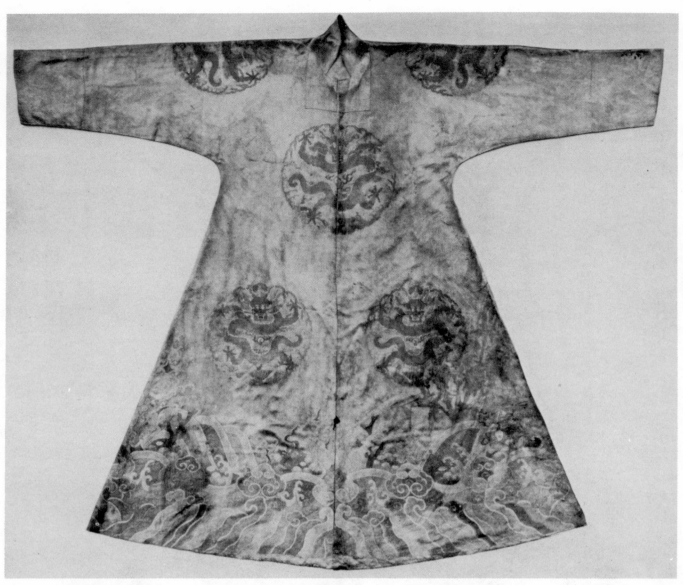

27. Giant Wave robe, from the tomb of Kuo Ch'in Wang (d. 1738). Brocaded satin. William Rockhill Nelson Gallery of Art, Kansas City

28. Bat Medallion robe, from the tomb of Kuo Ch'in Wang (d. 1738). Embroidered satin. The Metropolitan Museum. Anonymous gift, 1943

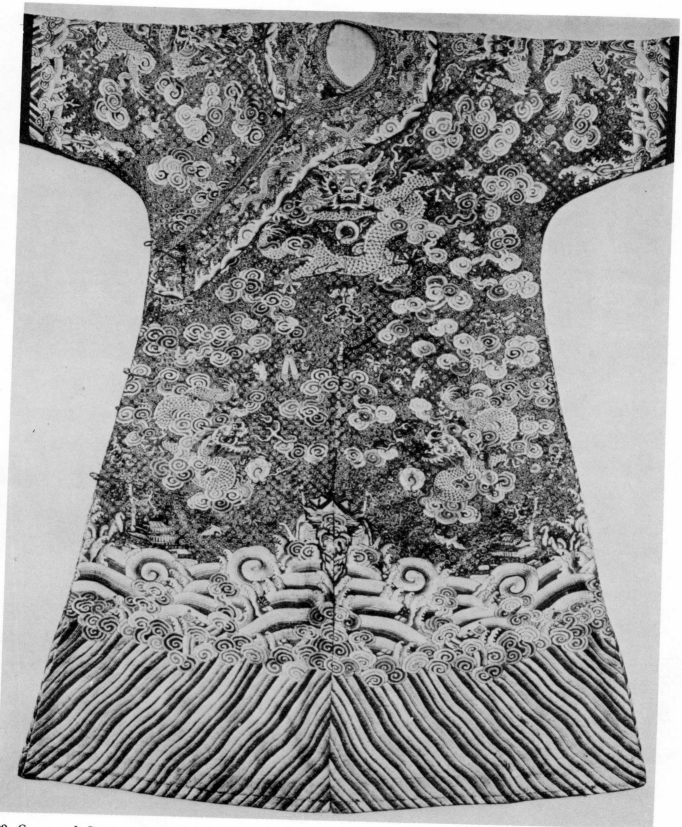

29. Crane and Gate or *T'ing Ling-wei* robe, from the tomb of Kuo Ch'in Wang (d. 1738). Embroidered satin.
The Minneapolis Institute of Arts

30. **Twelve-symbol emperor's robe, Ch'ien Lung period. Silk tapestry (*k'o ssŭ*). The Minneapolis Institute of Arts**

31. Robe with hurricane wave variant, Ch'ien Lung period. Embroidered satin. The Minneapolis Institute of Arts

32. Twelve-symbol emperor's robe, Ch'ien Lung period. Silk tapestry (*k'o ssŭ*). The Minneapolis Institute of Arts

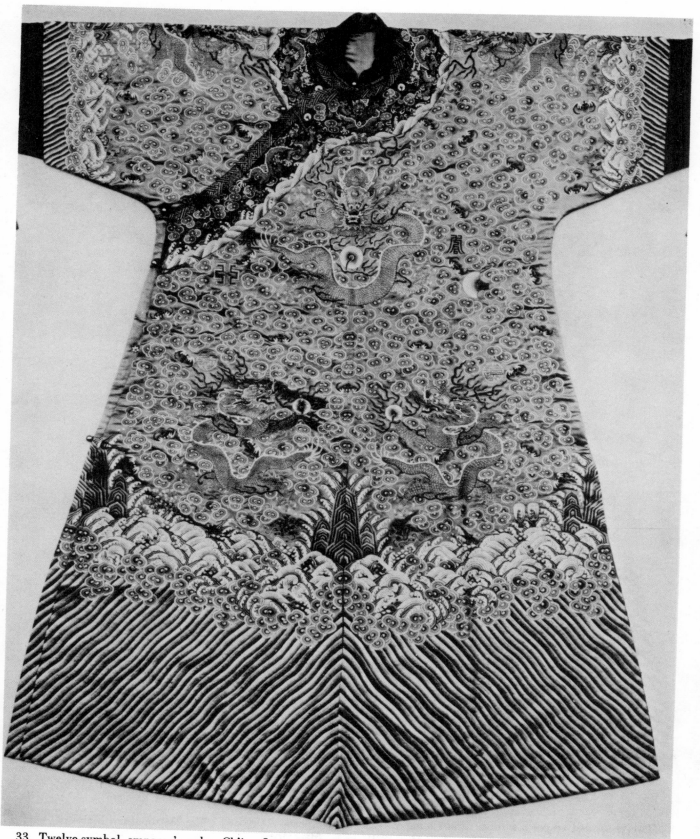

33. Twelve-symbol emperor's robe, Ch'ien Lung period. Embroidered satin. The Minneapolis Institute of Arts

34. Twelve-symbol emperor's robe, Chia Ch'ing period. Silk tapestry (*k'o ssŭ*). The Metropolitan Museum. Gift of Mrs. William H. Bliss, 1928

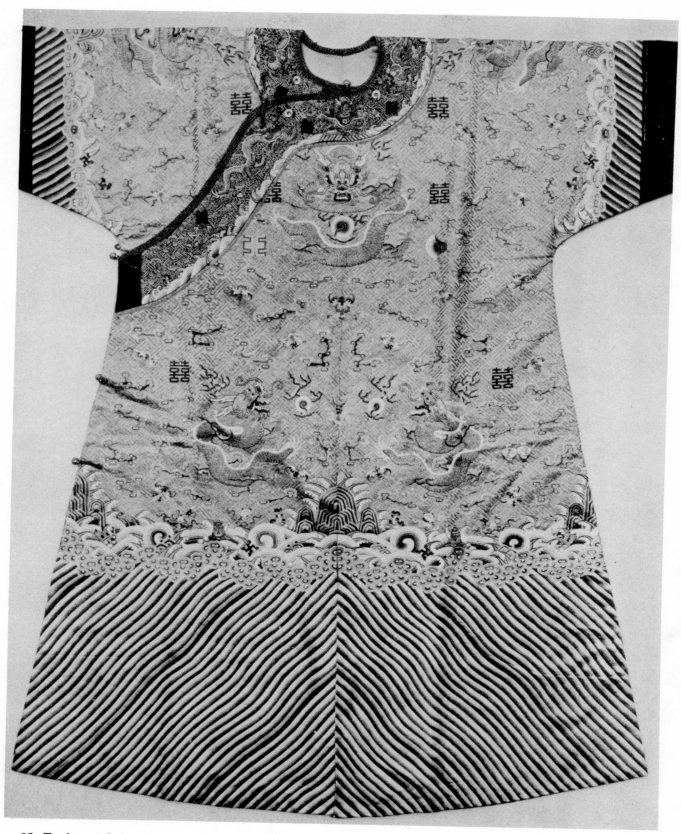

35. Twelve-symbol emperor's robe, Chia Ch'ing period. Embroidered satin. The Minneapolis Institute of Arts

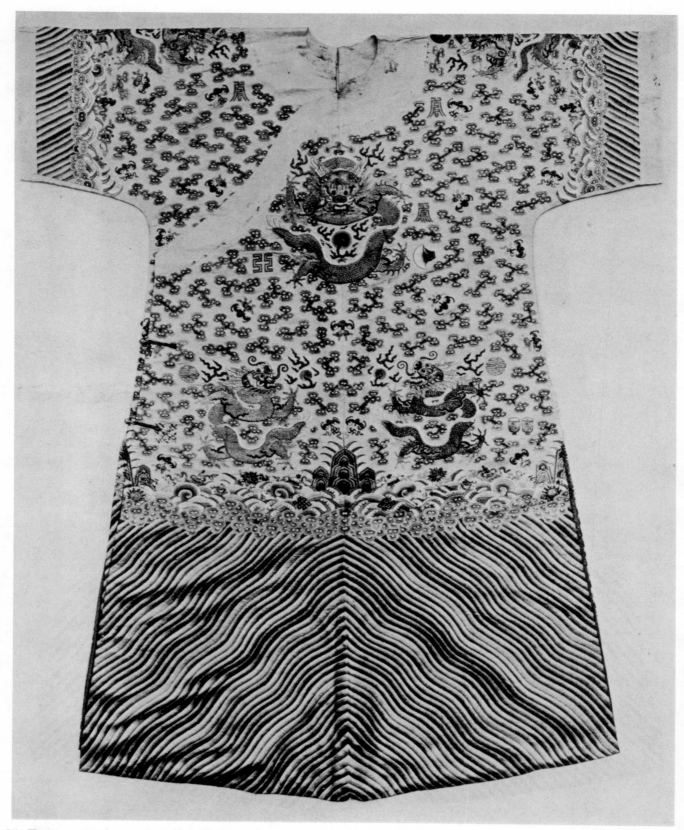

36. Twelve-symbol emperor's robe, Tao Kuang period. Embroidered silk twill. The Metropolitan Museum. Gift of Alice Boney, 1945

37. Twelve-symbol imperial robe, hurricane wave variant, Tao Kuang period. Embroidered satin. The Minneapolis Institute of Arts

道光十五年歲次乙未穀旦

38. Hanging, Tao Kuang period (dated 1835). Embroidered satin. The Minneapolis Institute of Arts

39. Twelve-symbol emperor's robe of state, attributed to T'ung Chih period. Embroidered gauze. The Metropolitan Museum. Purchase, Rogers Fund, 1945

40. Empress's robe, T'ung Chih or Kuang Hsü period. Embroidered satin with pearl and coral dragons. The Metropolitan Museum. Gift of Robert E. Tod, 1929

41. Informal robe which may have belonged to the Empress Dowager Tz'ŭ Hsi, Kuang Hsü period. Silk tapestry (*k'o ssŭ*). The Metropolitan Museum. Gift of Mrs. William H. Bliss, 1927

42. Imperial robe, Kuang Hsü period. Silk tapestry (*k'o ssŭ*). The Metropolitan Museum. Gift of Mrs. John D. Rockefeller, Jr., 1937

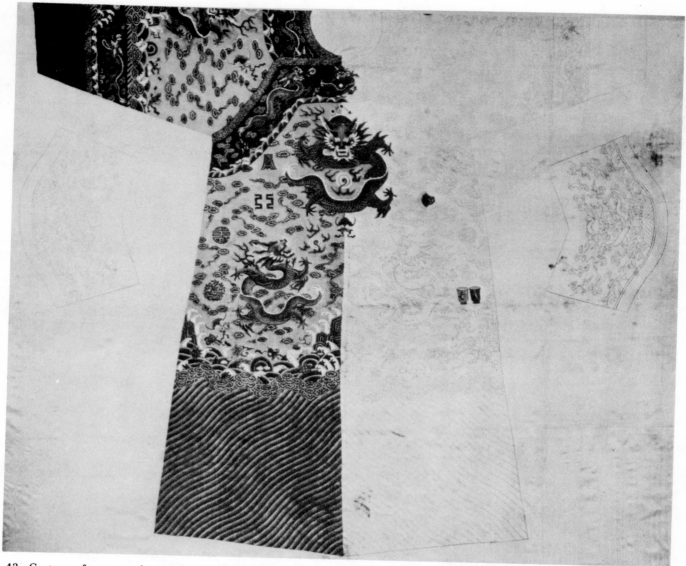

43. Cartoon for a twelve-symbol robe, Kuang Hsü or Hsüan T'ung period. Painted and stamped silk. The William Rockhill Nelson Gallery of Art, Kansas City

44. Imperial robe, probably Hsüan T'ung period. Brocaded silk twill. The Minneapolis Institute of Arts

45. Buddhist priest robe, late K'ang Hsi period. Silk tapestry (*k'o ssŭ*). The Metropolitan Museum. Bequest of William Christian Paul, 1930

46. Taoist priest robe, late K'ang Hsi period. Silk tapestry (*k'o ssŭ*). The Metropolitan Museum. Gift of Florance Waterbury, 1943

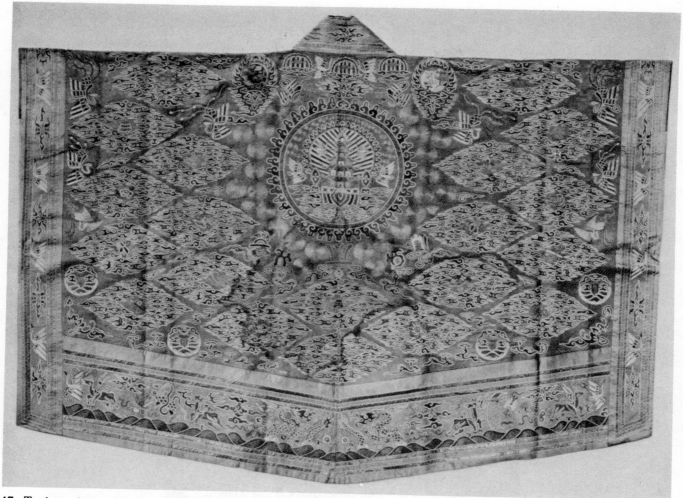

47. Taoist priest robe, inscribed the eleventh year of Ch'ien Lung's reign (1746), made for the head of a Taoist monastery, the Chen Jên Fu ("Pope"), Chang of Lung Hu Shan. Embroidered satin. The Minneapolis Institute of Arts

48. Taoist priest robe, secondary type, inscribed the eleventh year of Hsien Fêng's reign (1861). Embroidered satin. The Minneapolis Institute of Arts

49. Scroll of the Hundred or Five Hundred Lohan, stamped with Ch'ien Lung's seals. Silk tapestry (*k'o ssŭ*). The Minneapolis Institute of Arts

50. Theatrical robe for a court lady or dancer, late K'ang Hsi period. Embroidered satin. The Metropolitan Museum. Purchase, Rogers Fund, 1930

51. Theatrical robes for court ladies or dancers, late K'ang Hsi period. Embroidered satin. The Metropolitan Museum. Purchase, Rogers Fund, 1930

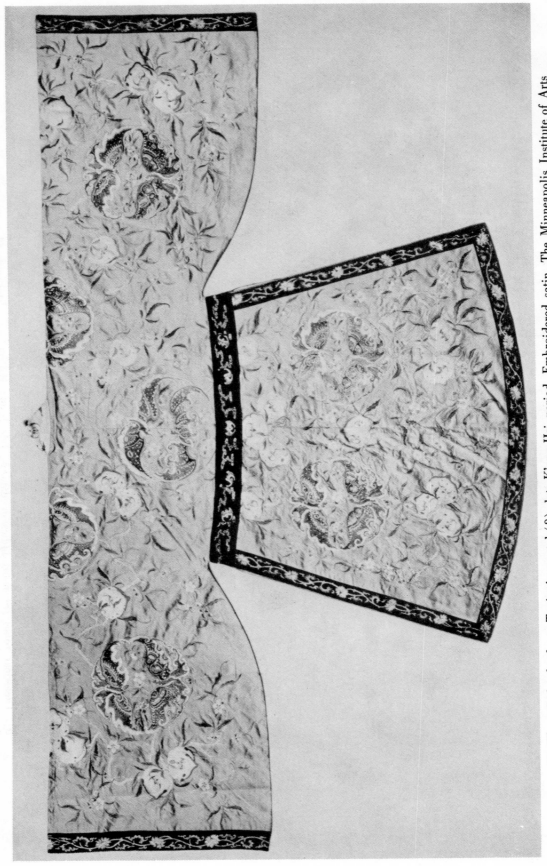

52. Theatrical robe for a Taoist immortal (?), late K'ang Hsi period. Embroidered satin. The Minneapolis Institute of Arts

53. Theatrical robe for a warrior, late K'ang Hsi period. Imported velvet and brocade with appliquéd details. The Metropolitan Museum. Purchase, Rogers Fund, 1930

54. Emperor's robe of state, Tao Kuang period. Embroidered satin. The Minneapolis Institute of Arts

55. Imperial hanging, K'ang Hsi period.   Brocaded satin.   The Minneapolis Institute of Arts

56. Imperial hanging (one of pair), K'ang Hsi period. Silk tapestry (*k'o ssŭ*). The Metropolitan Museum. Gift of Mrs. John F. Seamon, 1925

Metropolitan Museum of Art
Publications in Reprint

Egyptological Titles

Davies, Norman de Garis
The Tomb of Ken-Amun at Thebes (2 vols. in 1)
(Metropolitan Museum of Art Egyptian Expedition Publications, Vol. V: 1930)

Davies, Norman de Garis
The Tomb of Nefer-Hotep at Thebes (2 vols. in 1)
(Metropolitan Museum of Art Egyptian Expedition Publications, Vol. IX: 1933)

Davies, Norman de Garis
The Tomb of Rekh-Mi-Re at Thebes (2 vols. in 1)
(Metropolitan Museum of Art Egyptian Expedition Publications, Vol. XI: 1943)

Hayes, William C.
The Burial Chamber of the Treasurer Sobk-Mose from Er-Rizeikat
(Metropolitan Museum of Art Papers, No. 9: 1939)

Hayes, William C.
Glazed Tiles from a Palace of Ramesses II at Kantir
(Metropolitan Museum of Art Papers, No. 3: 1937)

Hayes, William C.
Ostraka and Name Stones from the Tomb of Sen-Mut (No. 71) at Thebes
(Metropolitan Museum of Art Egyptian Expedition Publications, Vol. XV: 1942)

Hayes, William C.
The Texts in the Mastabeh of Se'n-Wosret-Ankh at Lisht
(Metropolitan Museum of Art Egyptian Expedition Publications, Vol. XII: 1937)

Mace, Arthur C. and Winlock, Herbert E.
The Tomb of Senebtisi at Lisht
(Metropolitan Museum of Art Egyptian Expedition Publications, Vol. I: 1916)

White, Hugh G. Evelyn
The Monasteries of the Wadi 'N Natrun (3 vols.)
(Metropolitan Museum of Art Egyptian Expedition Publications, Vols. II, VII and VIII: 1926-1933)

> **New Coptic Texts from the Monastery of Saint Macarius** (1926)
> **The History of the Monasteries of Nitria and of Scetis,** ed. by Walter Hauser (1932)
> **The Architecture and Archaeology,** ed. by Walter Hauser (1933)

Schiller, A. Arthur
Ten Coptic Legal Texts

> (Metropolitan Museum of Art, Dept. of Egyptian Art Publications,
> Vol. II: 1932)

Winlock, Herbert E.
The Temple of Rameses I at Abydos (2 vols. in 1)

> (Metropolitan Museum of Art Papers, No. 1, Pt. 1 and No. 5, 1921-1937)
>> **Bas-Reliefs from the Temple of Rameses I at Abydos** (1921)
>> **The Temple of Ramesses I at Abydos** (1937)

Winlock, Herbert E.
Materials Used at the Embalming of King Tut-Ankh-Amun

> (Metropolitan Museum of Art Papers, No. 10: 1941)

Winlock, H. E.; Crum, W. E.; and White, Hugh G. Evelyn
The Monastery of Epiphanius at Thebes (2 vols.)

> (Metropolitan Museum of Art Egyptian Expedition Publications, Vols.
> III and IV: 1926)
>> **The Archaeological Material,** by H. E. Winlock;
>> **The Literary Material,** by W. E. Crum
>> **Coptic Ostraca and Papyri,** by W. E. Crum;
>> **Greek Ostraca and Papyri,** by H. G. E. White

Winlock, Herbert E.; White, Hugh G. Evelyn; and Oliver, James H.
The Temple of Hibis in El Khargeh Oasis (2 vols. in 1)

> (Metropolitan Museum of Art Egyptian Expedition Publications, Vols. XIII
> and XIV: 1938-1941)
>> **The Excavations,** by H. E. Winlock (1941)
>> **Greek Inscriptions,** by H. G. E. White and James H. Oliver (1938)

Winlock, Herbert E.
The Tomb of Queen Meryet-Amun at Thebes

> (Metropolitan Museum of Art Egyptian Expedition Publications, Vol. VI:
> 1932)

Winlock, Herbert E.
The Treasure of El Lahun

> (Metropolitan Museum of Art, Dept. of Egyptian Art Publications,
> Vol. IV: 1934)

Miscellaneous Titles

Avery, C. Louise
An Exhibition of Early New York Silver (1931)

Clouzot, Henri and Morris, Frances
Painted and Printed Fabrics (1927)

Grancsay, Stephen V.
The Armor of Galiot De Genouilhac
 (Metropolitan Museum of Art Papers, No. 4: 1937)

Grinnell, Isabel Hoopes
Greek Temples (1943)

Halsey, R. T. Haines
Catalogue of an Exhibition of Silver used in New York, New Jersey, and the South (1911)

Howe, Winifred E.
A History of The Metropolitan Museum of Art (1913)

Life in America
 A Special Loan Exhibition of Paintings Held During the Period of the New York World's Fair, April 24 to October 29 (1939)

Metropolitan Museum Studies, Vol. V, Part I (1934)

Myres, John L.
Handbook of The Cesnola Collection of Antiquities from Cyprus (1914)

Priest, Alan
Chinese Sculpture in The Metropolitan Museum of Art (1944)

Priest, Alan
Costumes from the Forbidden City (1945)

Scherer, Margaret R.
About the Round Table: King Arthur in Art and Literature (1945)

The Bulletin of The Metropolitan Museum of Art, 1905-1942
 With Cumulative Index (38 vols.)